CW01664516

Handling with Integrity When Preaching

Margaret Cooling
Preacher and Writer

GROVE BOOKS LIMITED
RIDLEY HALL RD CAMBRIDGE CB3 9HU

Contents

Acknowledgments

This booklet is a development of a series of lectures at Emmanuel Theological College residential weekends and I would like to express my thanks to the students who helped shaped my thinking by their responses.

First Impression September 2024
ISSN 1365-490X
ISBN 978 1 78827 413 5

1 Introduction

Being a virtuous preacher in relationship to the way we handle the Bible concerns the attitudes we bring to texts and the virtues we engage with when we interpret them. This is important for every reader of the Bible, but it is particularly important for preachers whose handling of texts becomes public in preaching.

In this book I draw on the work of Kevin Vanhoozer[1] and Richard Briggs but develop their insights in my own way in relation to preaching.[2] Both Briggs and Vanhoozer detail virtues and attitudes that people bring to texts and how the inclinations of our hearts and minds affect our approach and understanding. I have used some of the virtues they discuss as headings to explore the issues that arise for preachers. The virtues selected are those most pertinent to interpreting Scripture but they are also qualities that mark the Christian life. I have covered these virtues separately; they are, however, interconnected:

Love expressed in patience and loving attention
Honesty that builds trust
Humility that leaves us open and receptive
Responsibility exercised in wisdom
Honour and respect

These biblical virtues act as a framework through which we read the Bible. Interpreting a text is a moral as well as an intellectual activity; the two cannot be separated. How we live and how we read Scripture are related. But a word of caution: although the words for these virtues are familiar, they are often described differently in the Bible from the way they are understood in modern Western cultures. The Bible also brings a different dimension to virtues by being rooted in the relationship with God. Biblical virtues are not abstract; they are grounded in the narratives of a people and their practice in everyday life. Unless we are intentional about the attitudes we bring to the text, we might unwittingly import an understanding of a virtue that is alien to the Bible.

Throughout this book I give short examples from sermons. Those indicated in brackets can be found on www.preachingthatshows.com

2 Love

Love: A Biblical Perspective

The biblical concept of love differs from the modern concept, which tends to be an umbrella word for anything from being nice to sacrificial action on behalf of another. Love in the Bible encompasses compassion, faithfulness, mercy, loyalty and kindness, summed up in the Hebrew word *hesed*. Love is also delighting in another person and desiring another's good (Phil 2.3–4). Paul labels love (Greek *agapē*) the chief of virtues (1 Cor 13.13) and it is described as God's defining quality: 'God is love' (1 John 4.8).

For Jesus, love of God and neighbour summed up the law and the prophets (Mark 12.28–31). The ultimate definition of love is the love that took Jesus to the cross (Gal 2.20). Paul gives a detailed characterization of love in 1 Cor 13, describing it in terms of what it is (patient, kind, hopeful etc) and what it is not (proud, selfish, envious etc). Love involves the whole person: mind, soul, body and heart (Deut 6.5; Matt 22.37). The prophet Hosea's marriage reflects God's persevering love (Hosea 1–3). The story of Ruth shows different aspects of love, expressed by Ruth, Naomi and Boaz. The story of the Good Samaritan demonstrates love by an 'outsider' (Luke 10.25–37). The story of Jacob and Rachel shows the patience of love (Gen 29.18). Biblical texts concerning love shape our understanding of this virtue and how it is practised.

Double Love and Charitable Reading

Augustine of Hippo saw love as the virtue needed to read Scripture rightly. He uses the word charity (*caritas*) to describe love that is anchored in the text and builds up the double love of God and neighbour. A loving interpretation is not without challenge, for a loving reading is about being all that we can be in Christ and that means facing change as we all fall short. Love does not ignore problems in the text, but it describes the attitude and the goal with which these problems are addressed. However, wisdom is needed to discern what a loving/charitable interpretation might be in any particular context.

Charitable reading involves loyalty to the text and respect for the author but there can be a tension between doing justice to a text and reading charitably. It is not always obvious how a particular text can build up the love of God and neighbour. There is no formula for resolving this tension; the preacher works with the tension in each case. Loving readings of Scripture also bless but the preacher needs wisdom to decide the nature of the blessing. The way a preacher uses Scripture to bless in one situation might not be appropriate in another. Not all charitable readings of a text are the same; texts are complex and have depth, leaving room for more than one reading.

A loving reading engages with difficulties in the text in a way that builds up the congregation. Even when a text is difficult, a charitable reading can sometimes be found; Psalm 137 is one such instance. Verses 8 and 9 are often avoided with their violent imagery. However, they are the words of a people who have experienced horror; they are being honest concerning their own feelings about the perpetrators. The psalm does not give the people the right to exact this justice or say that this is God's view, but it does free people to be honest with God.[3]

Example

A charitable reading of the story of Jacob's ladder may focus on the parts of the text that contrast Jacob and God (Gen 28.10–22). Jacob lays down conditions for accepting the Lord as his God (vv 20–22), whereas God makes unconditional promises (vv 13–15). God does not reject Jacob for laying down terms. God meets Jacob where he is, not where he should be but that does not mean God will leave him there. The preacher can focus on this aspect of the text and explore ways it could be used to encourage and bless a congregation. A less charitable reading might itemize Jacob's conditions, pointing out what is wrong with each, emphasizing that we should not bargain with God. Such a reading might make people feel guilty without showing a way forward.

Engagement

What might a charitable reading of Luke 3.1–18 look like? How could it build up love of God and neighbour and be used to bless a congregation? Look at the harshness of some of John's words and his practical advice in the light of his message of repentance and forgiveness. Verse 18 defines John's message as 'good news'; in what way is it good news?

Patient, Loving Attention

Paul describes love as patient and persevering (1 Cor 13.4, 7). Patience in the Bible is active rather than passive. Patience in preparation is working with the expectation that insight will come but allowing time for the text to unfold its meaning on its own terms. It is not bludgeoning a text into revealing its meaning because we are desperate for a sermon.

Allowing a text to unfold its meaning needs loving attention paid to the whole text, not just the 'spiritual bits.' Loving attention is a way of expressing the worth of a text as it is a form of attention that comes from the heart (Heb 2.1). Loving attention begins by putting aside the big questions such as 'What does this text mean?' The focus moves to ordinary things in the text: names, the weather, the landscape, the time and the body language. Ordinary questions are asked such as, 'What is happening?' 'How are people relating to each other?' 'What is daily life like?' This type of attention slows us down and brings the world of the text into focus. Questions concerning what is happening spiritually are left to last because people's relationship with God is affected by everyday material experiences, not just things we would label as spiritual. God can speak to us through these material elements of the text just as God addresses us through everyday experience in our lives.

Example

At the beginning of the story of Jacob's ladder (Gen 28.10–22) we are told the following information:

> Jacob left Beersheba and set out for Haran. When he reached a certain place, he stopped for the night because the sun had set. Taking one of the stones there, he put it under his head and lay down to sleep. (vv 10–11; NIV)

It is tempting to go straight to the dream (vv 12–15), the spiritual bit, but the details in the preceding verses are important. Jacob is young. He has fled from his home as his brother Esau wants to kill him for stealing his inheritance. He arrives at a clearing—a place with no name. He is alone and in strange territory. He has nothing, and a stone has to serve as a pillow (Gen 32.10). He is far from his family in Beersheba and not yet at his uncle's place in Haran, which is six hundred miles from home. It is dark. The text gives the impression that this is not a planned stop; the sun sets and Jacob stops where he is. All Jacob's securities have been taken away. He is out of all routines and away from all familiar things. This is when God speaks to him. This type of focus gives the situation and the characters the attention they deserve. It places value on all parts of the text by exploring how encounters with God sometimes happen when we are out of routines and in unfamiliar places. Such situations often make us feel vulnerable but that experience can make us more open to God.

Engagement

Read the story of the feeding of the four thousand (Matt 15.29–39). Pay attention to the whole text and what the words mean in real terms for the people in the story. What is involved in statements made in the passage? Translate the words into actions. For example, how do the people mentioned in vv 29–30 get up the mountain? In what ways does meaning arise from loving attention paid to these factors?

Attending to the Familiar

Paying loving attention to a text is difficult if it is familiar; our brain might register that we already know it and it becomes difficult to penetrate the film of familiarity. Preachers can feel like pond skater insects moving across the surface of a text. In order to attend to familiar parts of the Bible we have to defamiliarize the text and this involves patience and perseverance. Defamiliarizing involves reading the text in different versions, aloud and slowly. Another way to defamiliarize a text is to imagine a friend who is not a Christian hearing it. See yourself sitting next to them as the text is read in church. How would they hear it? If it is a narrative, think about it from the perspective of different characters in order to hear the text differently.

Example

Read Mark 5.21–43 from the perspective of the woman with a haemorrhage.

In your imagination, follow the woman as she sets out to follow Jesus. Think about the way she would walk, how she would hold her clothes. In your mind's eye 'see' people's reaction to her. In v 27 we are told the woman with a haemorrhage reaches out to touch Jesus' cloak. Verses 30–32 show us Jesus' response: he whips around and asks who touched him when he feels power go out of him. If we look closely at verse 33 it tells us where people are. The woman is kneeling at Jesus' feet and the disciples and the crowd surround them. Verse 35 is very clear that it is while Jesus is speaking to the woman that the messengers come to say that Jairus' daughter is dead. The woman is still at Jesus' feet. If Jesus heard that message so did she. How must she have felt! Did she wonder if stopping Jesus in order to be healed had led to the child's death? The woman would have been on the margins of society, Jairus was at its centre—a man of importance—but Jesus' compassion does not differentiate. Attending to the familiar from a different perspective can help us feel in a fresh way the love that crosses the lines that society makes.

Engagement

Read the Beatitudes and imagine a non-Christian friend sitting next to you (Matt 5.1–9). How would they hear this passage ? What might be their response? How might this exercise help you to prepare a sermon on this text?

3 Honesty

Honesty: A Biblical Perspective

Honesty is crucial in handling texts. In 2 Cor 4.2 Paul talks of handling the word of God without deception or distortion but openly setting out the truth. As preachers we are called to be honest witnesses: honest about what the text says, honest about the behaviour of people in the text and honest about the complexity of a text and the struggles of the Christian life. There is no room for pretending in the pulpit.

Honesty builds trust and provides the framework within which a preacher works. God's word is described as trustworthy (Ps 19.7). Trust is believing that there is something in the text to be understood and that God wills to communicate. We do not wrench meaning from a reluctant God. When the Bible talks of trusting in God and not relying on our own understanding, it does not mean that we shun study or critical scholarship (Prov 3.5–6). Trust in God builds the security and confidence that enables us to engage with scholarship. Not trusting our own understanding means that we can have a healthy acknowledgment of our fallen nature knowing that we need the renewal of our minds (Rom 12.2).

Honesty is closely related to being sincere and pure and it is associated with truth, which needs to be spoken with gentleness (Eph 4.15). Paul calls upon the Philippians to think on what is true and pure (Phil 4.8). Honesty is positive; it is an attitude of the heart not just the opposite of lies and deceit (Psa 15.2). The story of the call of Nathanael illustrates honesty; Jesus declared Nathanael to be a man without deceit (John 1.47). Naboth's vineyard is a story of false witness and dishonesty (1 Kgs 21). Jesus censured the Pharisees for not being honest in their interpretation of the commandment to honour parents (Mark 7.8–13). The story of Micaiah is the story of a prophet who refused to lie, who spoke the truth in a dangerous situation (1 Kgs 22; 2 Chron 18).

At its heart biblical truth is embodied in a person, Jesus, who described himself as the way, the truth and the life (John 14.6). The spirit leads people into truth (John 16.13), which is more than an intellectual understanding of doctrines; the Spirit enables people to respond to the truth that is Jesus.

Honesty About Where We Are Coming From

Every preacher comes to the Bible with the ideas they already have about a text—their pre-understandings and assumptions. No one comes to a text as a blank slate. Being honest means acknowledging pre-understandings as an initial step in preparation. This act of conscious acknowledgment has the potential to make us more receptive to the text. Many preachers come to the story of the woman who anointed Jesus with the assumption that she was a prostitute and that she had chosen that profession (Luke 7.36–50). The term 'sinner' and the woman's behaviour could indicate prostitution but that does not mean she chose that life. She might have been sold into prostitution or been driven to it by debt and destitution. We cannot assume prostitution was her choice. Are we sometimes too quick to assume sexual sin if it is a woman who is designated a sinner?

Example

The understandings we have about baptism and personal salvation might hinder our understanding of the baptism of whole households, which occurs a number of times in the New Testament: Lydia's household, the Philippian gaoler's household and the household of Stephanas (Acts 16.13–15, 30–33; 1 Cor 1.16). We should be honest about such texts. A household could include children, extended family and possibly servants. This does not mean we abandon belief in personal salvation; it does mean that we research this practice and what 'household' baptism might mean in this context. We cannot assume that every person in a household made a personal commitment before they were baptized.

Engagement

Without looking at the text, think about the Parable of the Prodigal Son (Luke 15.11–32). Write down what you assume to be important about the text and its message. Now read the text slowly. Are your assumptions justified? What part of the text have you emphasized? What has moved out of focus? How might someone from a different background have read this parable and emphasized different aspects of it? When you have done this, you might like to look at Mark Allan Powell's research on how people in different cultures read this parable.[4]

Honesty about Biblical Characters

Biblical characters may be in a book entitled 'Holy Bible,' but some behave in a very unholy fashion. The Bible is remarkably frank about the failings of biblical characters such as Noah and David. It presents us with fallible characters who are a mixture of good and bad, as we are. As preachers we need to make honest judgments about biblical characters. Not being honest about this could result in the congregation viewing biblical characters as beyond judgment, people who live in a spiritual neverland where accepted standards do not apply. The characters become unreal and we cannot learn from them.

To be honest about characters means avoiding simplistic presentations of people as good or bad. Good people sometimes do bad things and bad people sometimes do good things. Esau gets a bad press in the Bible, with some justification (Heb 12.16), but Esau also shows remarkable forgiveness when he meets the brother who cheated him out of his inheritance (Gen 33.4).

Example

Abram twice described Sarai as his sister rather than his wife, which led to her being taken away by other men (Gen 12.11–20; 20.1–18). The text is clear that this was an act of self-preservation on Abram's part (Gen 12.12–13). Little thought seems to have been given to the consequences for Sarai. If the preacher is honest about the behaviour of biblical characters, it gives people permission to respond appropriately. Facing Abram's failings but recognizing that even this did not destroy his relationship with God gives hope.

Engagement

Read Gen 16.1–6 and an accompanying commentary. What would a truthful picture of Sarai look like in a sermon?

Honesty about Faith and Life

We read the Bible believing that its words relate to us and how we live as Christians—they tell the truth about life. The way we present the Bible in sermons equally needs to tell the truth about life and faith, facing the complexities of living as a Christian. Simplistic versions of the Christian faith can be disastrous pastorally as they can set up guilt and failure when people try to put them into practice.

Example

Sermons about anxiety usually quote a series of verses on the subject. Most of these are predictable: 'Do not worry about your life…' (Luke 12.22); 'Do not be anxious about anything…' (Phil 4.6); 'Cast all your anxiety on him because he cares for you' (1 Pet 5.7) etc. Just knowing these verses does not necessarily relieve anxiety; it can make anxiety worse, for now the anxious feel guilty about not trusting God.

Rather than just exhorting people not to be anxious, a sermon can acknowledge the complexity of the subject. God created us with a flight or fight mechanism that keeps us safe. Anxiety is part of this; it is looking ahead for potential threats. It is not, therefore, surprising that we find it difficult to eschew anxiety and trust God. Personality factors are also involved. People who are not anxious are not necessarily more spiritual, they might just be people with a more relaxed personality. The anxious person is not necessarily less spiritual, they might have already given God a lot of their anxiety but are still struggling with some worries. The sermon can acknowledge this struggle by including people such as Elijah who was afraid and sections of the psalms that express anguish and fear (*eg* Psa 31) as well as the standard texts. Beware the sentence that begins, 'You just...' and offers a simple answer to a complex issue.

Engagement

What biblical texts spring to mind when you think about anger? Now think about the complexities of anger: is it affected by personality types? Are there different types of anger? What are the differing situations that evoke anger? Are there times when not being angry would be wrong? What other texts might you draw on to reflect a little of the complexity of the subject?

Staying True to a Text

Preachers have a responsibility to stay true to a text. This is more than just repeating the content and applying it, it is a creative process that has three aspects that Vanhoozer labels: matter, force and momentum.[5]

- Maintaining the same matter as the text: reflecting its content and subject matter. It is staying close to what the text is about, including events, issues, doctrines and people. However, by itself content is not enough.
- Maintaining the same force as the text: its energy, what the words are doing. For example, the text might promise, command, comfort or correct. To stay true to the text a sermon needs to do what the text does, rather than just repeating what it says. To turn an encouraging text into a judging sermon would not be true to its force. The full force of the text needs to be felt when preparing, even if that text is violent or disturbing. When we preach we can be honest about how we felt when preparing but wisdom is needed concerning how much of that force is retained in the sermon and how it can be situated within the greater force of God's love. With violent and sexually explicit texts pastoral concerns are uppermost concerning how they are approached in a sermon. Graphic detail is not needed.
- Maintaining the momentum of the text: following the direction of thought of the text and carrying this through to how it is practised. This means making sure the text is not taken out of context and interpreting it within the overarching story of redemption. In Jer

29.11 God speaks of 'plans to prosper you.' It was a promise given to a nation in exile. It would not be following the direction of the text if it was used as a promise of individual prosperity today.

Example

The subject matter of Rom 8.32–39 is the inalienable love of God in the face of all that life throws at us (Rom 8.38–39). Its force or energy is one of triumph and assurance through the love of God in Christ (Rom 8.32–35). The sermon can preserve this force by detailing some of the things we face in life today and how they cannot separate us from God's love. This preserves the momentum of the text to provide assurance. A sermon that majored on the effects of sin using this text would lose this force and momentum.

Engagement

Read 1 Sam 16.1–13. What is the matter of this text? List its content and subject matter. What is the force and energy of the text? Write down what you think the text is seeking to do. What is its momentum, its direction of thought? How could the force of the text and its direction be preserved in the sermon?

4

Humility

Humility: A Biblical Perspective

Humility has had a chequered history; in the Greek world it was often equated with being servile and of little importance. For Aristotle it was not a virtue. In Christianity, the word gained a new life, and humility became the virtue that allows us to see ourselves as we truly are in relation to God and others (Rom 12.3). Christ's humility became an example for all Christians (Phil 2.5–8). For Augustine of Hippo, it was the chief of virtues. This type of humility is not a lack of self-esteem or a denial of abilities or achievements, it is an honest assessment of ourselves before God. The centurion whose servant Jesus healed showed humility: he accepted his own power was limited compared to that of Jesus (Luke 7.1–10). Humility also lies in being willing to do things for others that might be considered inferior. The story of Jesus washing his disciples' feet illustrates this aspect of humility (John 13.1–17).

Humility before a text can make us more receptive and open. Receptivity and openness are about a willingness to listen and being open in heart and mind towards God's word. Christians are called to receive the kingdom like a child (Luke 18.15–17) with receptive hearts (Jas 1.21). The story of Peter and Cornelius is a story of openness (Acts 10).

Humility in Our Attitude to the Text

Humility does not function on its own, it is exercised in conjunction with other interpretive virtues such as honesty and wisdom. Humility means we sit prayerfully under a text, not over it. This applies to our attitude to the whole Bible, through which we seek to hear the voice of God. We do not master the text; the text masters us. Mastery gives us control, leaving the object passive, which is inappropriate when reading the Bible. The text does not lie before us like a dead body before a forensic scientist; it is a living word. We enter into a dialogue with a text and that dialogue can be robust. However, it is entered into prayerfully and is the expression of a lived faith. Humility does not mean unquestioning agreement. We question the text. It questions us.

Example

The structure of Ecclesiastes and its message has led to much debate. Some parts are positive and affirming of life and faith (Eccl 3.11; 7.11–12); other parts are negative and pessimistic (Eccl 1.8, 12–13; 4.2). Sometimes both optimism and pessimism are in the same chapter. The initial desire might be to try and master this unusual biblical book, but much is missed that way. An alternative approach is to immerse yourself in the text and let the questions arise that you want to ask and think about the questions the text is asking you.

Engagement

Read Ecclesiastes 1 slowly and prayerfully, immersing yourself in the chapter, without seeking to organize it or get points from it. As you read allow the questions you want to ask to emerge, then read it again, thinking about the questions God might be asking you through this chapter.

Humility and Thinking

Exercising humility when interpreting texts requires an attitude of dependence on God. This does not mean abdicating the work of thinking; it is deciding the attitude with which we think. Humility is also needed in relation to human understanding. We are fallen but redeemed creatures who are fallible. Although much has been revealed to us through Christ there is still mystery. In Paul's words we 'see through a glass darkly' (1 Cor 13.12 KJV). This need not lead to uncertainty or lack of confidence; it might lead to a rejection of dogmatic attitudes and arrogance.

Humility means we have to let go of the image of the preacher who has clarity on every issue and is able to answer all questions with the appropriate Bible verse. That is not the nature of either the Bible or life. Some biblical texts are open-ended, others finish with possibilities or questions and some things are never resolved or are left unsaid. Despite this, the sermon can bring assurance and what Lesslie Newbigin calls 'proper confidence,' which he describes as the confidence of someone who has heard God's call and responded as a disciple, rather than a claim to have unquestionable knowledge.[6]

Example

There is mystery around the operation of God's will (Eph 1.5, 11) and human freedom (2 Cor 5.10; Rev 22.12). No answer is given to the problem of pain in the Book of Job or why the wicked prosper (Psa 73.3–6). The Book of Jonah ends with a question (Jonah 4. 10–11) and the Parable of the Unjust Steward raises more questions than answers (Luke 16.1–9).

Engagement

Think about the virtues listed in the introduction. In what ways does humility underpin these other virtues?

A Humble and Receptive Attitude

The preacher is called to be receptive to the subject of the text, to commit to staying long enough in the text to see what is really there rather than making quick judgments. A teachable attitude is needed. This particularly applies to difficult texts. Instant judgments close us down and we cease to be receptive. Briggs advises 'holding your nerve' before difficult texts; this allows the reader to follow where the text leads, even if it feels strange or unacceptable.[7] The text is given a full hearing before any judgment is made. This does not make difficulties disappear, but it does mean we listen fully before our responses are expressed. Humble receptivity means coming to the text willing to be transformed.

A similar attitude of receptivity is also needed for texts we classify as 'straight-forward.' That instant, positive judgment can also close us down. However well we know a text, the Holy Spirit can still lead us into new insights. Over time our understanding can change and deepen if we remain receptive.

Example

In chapter two on love, Ps 137.8–9 was used as an example of a difficult text. The nature of this text can cause an instant negative reaction. It rightly makes us recoil. Humility means we temporarily suspend judgment in the belief that even this terrible text can teach us. As we engage with the text and its historical background, we realize the situation that called forth such anger. This text shows us that we can vent anger and despair, for we cannot change until we have faced what we truly feel, but that does not mean God agrees or wants to leave us there. Love, humility and receptivity can work together.

Engagement

Think about a text you have preached on in the past. If you were to preach on that text again what would remain the same? What would you change? How has your understanding changed and deepened over time?

Open and Receptive to Other Perspectives

We are each situated in a particular place, time and culture that influences how we understand texts. Most of us also sit somewhere within a Christian tradition (Evangelical, Pentecostal, Sacramental etc), that influences us too. Humility before a text means that we remain open to other perspectives. It can be too cosy to read only within our own time, culture and tradition, consulting only 'safe' scholars. Reading outside our tradition, time and culture can bring insights and challenges. Widening our reading helps us to see a text in a new way. If we are receptive we can learn from a range of scholars, past and present.

Example

Protestant Christians put little emphasis on Holy Saturday, the time between the death of Jesus commemorated on Good Friday and the resurrection celebrated on the following Sunday. The Saturday was the Sabbath as noted in Luke when the followers of Jesus were gathered in grief (Luke 23.54–56). Holy Saturday is important in the Orthodox tradition. Loss is faced which intensifies the joy of Easter. Maybe this helps Christians to understand a little of what the disciples went through. This is expressed in the following extract.

> Saturday: the day sandwiched between the drama of death
> and the joy of new life. A nothing day.
> A day we can bear because we know what is coming.
> Not so for the disciples, not so for Mary.
> For us, Saturday is a stepping stone to joy,
> but not for them; there was nothing to wait for,
> they did not know the ending.
>
> For us, Saturday is a gap to be spanned,
> a ravine to be bridged, a valley to be crossed.
> For us, the other side is in view. But not for them.
> For them, Saturday was a chasm,
> an abyss of sorrow no bridge could span.
> For them, there was no other side,
> no knowledge of Easter Sunday to made Saturday bearable.
> He was not gone for a little while, he was gone.
>
> (Sermon: *Holy Saturday*)

Engagement

In terms of understanding biblical texts, think of one thing that you have learned from other traditions, times or cultures.

Responsible Wisdom 5

Responsible Wisdom: A Biblical Perspective

Responsibility and accountability are found in the Bible in terms of human responsibility before God (Rom 14.12) and our responsibility in using our spiritual gifts (Rom 12.6–8). Preachers are called to a responsible handling of the Bible (2 Tim 2.15) for those who teach (and preach?) will be judged more strictly (Jas 3.1). This means we are not free to use the text in any way we want. We are accountable for what we preach. Exercising responsibility requires wisdom which is more than knowledge. Biblical wisdom is broad, being a matter of the mind and behaviour; it is both discernment and practice (Deut 34.9; Phil 1.9–10, Jas 3.13–18). Wisdom is living with the grain of Scripture and the grain of God's world. In preaching we draw on the wisdom of God reflected in the Bible (Prov 9.10). The wisdom we need is both a gift of God (Jas 1.5) and something we nurture and exercise (Jas 3.13).

A Responsible Relationship to the Text

The Bible has many metaphors for God's word: guide, light, sword and seed are just a few. It is easy to slip into using just a few familiar metaphors rather than explore the riches of biblical language in this area. The preacher needs wisdom to discern what the text is doing and decide what metaphor best describes how it is functioning.

There are other metaphors that might be helpful in describing the preacher's relationship to the text. Wayne Booth explores the metaphor of friendship. He makes the point that reading is a meeting of people—the author and reader. When writing about texts in general, Booth asks what sort of company a text offers us. Certain texts can function as good friends and he describes how we can dwell with these texts and let them show us a way of life that is profound, sensitive, curious, intense and generous. The text as friend can also correct and rebuke us as only true friends can. These texts can shape our desires and show us what life can be.[8]

Booth is aware that the friendship metaphor has limitations, but that is true of all metaphors, including biblical ones. Metaphors are always partial; they illuminate some aspects of a subject and hide others. Wisdom has to be exercised in how we use metaphors, for they can all be pressed too far. The friendship metaphor might have possibilities for our relationship to the Bible. The Bible talks of the friendship of the Lord and in reading the Bible we experience an encounter between us as readers, the author and God (Ps 25.14 NRSV; John 15.15). The text as friend means it ceases to be a thing that can be put at a distance; there is a more personal response and there is a responsibility to a friend. A friendship does not have to be equal and a strong friendship can withstand challenge and correction. As we read the Bible we can ask, 'What sort of company is this text offering me and my congregation?'

Another metaphor is hospitality, which views God, and the word of God, as host and us as guests. We are invited into God's story of redemption. We then have the responsibility to act appropriately as guests. As we read the Bible and prepare a sermon, we are guests in other people's stories and only after we have established this relationship do we make judgments. Another way of thinking about the hospitality metaphor is to think of ourselves as the hosts and we welcome a text into our lives and respond appropriately. The text is like a visitor from another culture and we have to take account of that when making the text welcome.

Example

Psalm 23 acts as a friend for many people. It is a text that often accompanies people throughout their life. This psalm is a friend through the dark times, with its assurance of God's presence. The story of Cain and Abel (Gen 4.1–15) can act as a critical friend, constantly reminding us that we are our brother's (and sister's) keeper and God cares about what happens to them (Gen 4.9–10). The story of the beheading of John the Baptist (Mark 6.14–29) may seem a strange type of friend but it is a text that reminds us that we live in a fallen world. We may speak the truth but that does not mean it will be well received. This text warns us that doing the right thing can have ruinous consequences. Jesus never said it would be easy.

Engagement

Think through the metaphors of friendship and hospitality / guest. How would these affect your relationship to the text? What are the positive aspects of these metaphors? What might be their limitations?

Accountable to the Meaning of a Text

Discerning the meaning of a text requires wisdom, for we are accountable to the text, which has rights and needs treating fairly. The text also has power; the Holy Spirit works through the text and its words can guide our understanding by the way it is written and by what is said. Both style and content matter. That does not mean rigid literalism: a text, like a musical score, may have a number of interpretations but the score exercises control concerning the range of credible interpretations. There is a degree of freedom in interpreting a text but wisdom is needed in the exercising of freedom for the text decides the limits. Preachers can exercise what Vanhoozer describes as 'creative fidelity,' being 'free yet faithful' when interpreting texts.[9] In coming to understanding, the author, the text and the reader—guided by the Spirit—work together towards meaning.

Example

The story of Mary and Martha is traditionally understood as Jesus affirming Mary's role of listening to him as 'the better part' when contrasted with Martha's active role (Luke 10.38–42). Traditionally the women have been seen as exemplifying contemplative and active types. N T Wright offers an alternative reading. Mary sits at Jesus' feet, the mode of someone learning from a rabbi, a distinctively male role occurring in the male part of the house—an active role. As a woman she should have been in the kitchen. Martha's complaint and Jesus' affirmation of Mary still stand but Martha's complaint is wider: her sister is flouting social norms and Jesus is affirming her behaviour.[10]

Engagement

Look up some commentaries on the story of Martha and Mary. To what extent are both the traditional reading and N T Wright's reading within the limits set by the text? Are both exercising 'creative fidelity'?

Responsibly Reflecting the Claim and Aim of a Text

Preachers have a responsibility to engage with the claims the text is making on us. The claim might come in the form of promises to be trusted, commands to obey and examples to follow or avoid. This is not a theoretical exercise, for claims require a response in Christian living. Discerning claims and finding a way forward in a modern context draws on wisdom's practical side. This is not about applying rigid formulae; it is about asking the right questions and Briggs sees wisdom as having a role in forming questions that lead to life.[11] The claim might involve a new way of thinking, believing, behaving or feeling. The way forward could be a new vision of our identity in Christ, new ways of relating to others or new insights into what we value. There might be an overall claim in a text or there could be several claims and wisdom is needed to make judgments between them. If claims appear to conflict or be unrelated, it might be possible to move to a point where one claim helps to make sense of the other.[12]

Related to this is the aim of a text. Only when we have journeyed with the text according to its aims can we begin to make judgments. Sometimes biblical authors state their aims (Luke 1.1–4); at other times, preachers have to exercise discernment to decide the aim from the author's directions that are expressed in the way the text is written.

Example

The story of the widow's offering sits in the context of Jesus' condemnation of lawyers who exploit vulnerable people such as widows (Mark 12.38–44). The text about lawyers contains a claim about corrupt behaviour, and this is followed by a text about a widow who gave what little she had. The claim about corrupt behaviour comes in the form of a negative example, the claim about giving comes in the form of a positive example. The claims might look unrelated but the first claim helps us to interpret the second (the widow's offering). She gives sacrificially but she should never have been so poor! She stands as an example of what happens in a society where people like the lawyers neglect God's commands to care for the vulnerable.

Engagement

Read the following texts: Neh 5.1–12; Gal 6.1–4. In each case discern the claim the text is making on the reader and note its form.

Responsibly Reflecting the Mood of a Text

Wisdom is needed to discern the mood of a text, its overall atmosphere. A text might have a joyful mood or a gloomy one. The mood of a text is a factor in deciding the mood of the sermon but it is not the only factor, for pastoral concerns and context come into play. It would be inappropriate for the angry mood of Jer 20.7–18 to create an angry sermon. The mood of the sermon works with the mood of the text but it does not have to mirror it. A sermon on Jeremiah 20 could acknowledge Jeremiah's feelings and face the times when we are angry with God or despair but the sermon's overall mood could be reflective and trace the changing mood of Jeremiah.

Example

Unlike modern films about the death of Jesus, Mark's account of the crucifixion of Jesus has a very restrained mood (Mark 15.22–25). There are no details of nails and blood. There are no sounds of physical agony. A mood of restrained grief would work with the text as in the example that follows.

Soldiers dice, oblivious to the misery.
Life goes on despite the agony—
now as then—in his pain and ours.
We feel that time should stand still to salute anguish.
The world should bow its head in acknowledgment of grief.
But children still play, work still has to be done,
the body still demands food,
soldiers still dice.

(Sermon: *Crucifixion: Too Much*)

Engagement

Drawing on just one gospel, locate three texts and indicate their mood.

6

Honour and Respect

Honour and Respect: A Biblical Perspective

It is difficult to separate honour and respect for they are closely related but not identical. The modern use of the word 'respect' covers many aspects of the biblical term 'honour.' Some versions of the Bible translate certain instances of the Greek word for honour as 'respect.' Compare 1 Pet 2.17 in the King James Version with the New International Version:

> Show proper respect to everyone, love the family of believers, fear God, honour the emperor. (NIV 2011)
>
> Honour all men. Love the brotherhood. Fear God. Honour the king. (KJV)

The Greek word for honour occurs twice in this verse but the NIV translates one of them as respect. Paul exhorts Christians to pay both honour and respect where it is due (Rom 13.7 NIV, NRSV). The biblical words for honour and respect denote glory, value, reverence, awe and esteem.

One Old Testament word for honour comes from a root word meaning heavy. This connotation exists in English when we talk of not treating a person or thing lightly. Primarily, honour is paid to God (Rev 4.11) but also to others (Rom 12.10). Children are commanded to honour their parents (Exod 20.12). Christians are commanded to treat everyone with respect (1 Pet 2.17a); all people are made in the image of God (Gen 1.27). That does not mean judgments are not made, for that image is marred. Making appropriate judgments can be a sign of respect, for it is treating people as fully human and responsible.

Honouring Characters

The people of the Bible are not pegs on which to hang spiritual or moral points, they are more than that and deserve treating respectfully. Biblical characters are people in their own right who laugh and cry, love and hate. They should not be dropped from a text once the meaning has been established, as if they were just the means of delivery. If characters are treated seriously, they are more likely to resonate with the congregation. However, there is sometimes little information about a character. If this is the case, preachers can draw on other texts that are related or share a comparable situation. They can research the background to understand the character in their context and draw on appropriate shared human experience.

Example

In Phil 4.2–3 Paul tells of two Christians in Philippi who have differed over something that was serious enough to need another person to mediate. We are only given basic information about Euodia and Syntyche, but it is enough to begin to picture them as people. Paul honours these women as front-line workers. He uses a word that has associations with the gladiatorial games to describe how these women 'struggled beside him.' They were gladiators for the gospel. Acts 16 fills in some details about the situation in Philippi. It was a dangerous place to be a Christian; Paul and Silas were beaten and imprisoned there (Acts 16.22–24). These are brave women. There was a small 'church' in Philippi that met in Lydia's house (Acts 16.40). These women would not have been able to move churches because they could not get on. Preachers can draw on appropriate human experience of disagreement and needing help to heal the breach. The picture of these women begins to build.

Engagement

How could you preach on Matt 1.18–25 in a way that brings out the character of Joseph? We are only told one thing about Joseph's character but look at his actions, explore the background, and imagine what Joseph's actions would have cost him in his culture.

Honouring the Genre

Honouring the genre of a text means taking account of its style and form, not just its content. Psalms cannot be treated in the same way as an epistle. In life we approach texts with the expectations appropriate to their genre. We do not read a shopping list in the same way as we read poetry. It honours a text when we read it according to the rules and expectations of its genre. The psalms are poetry for a reason. They speak to us through imagery, rhythm and sound patterns. They use language in a way that speaks to both mind and heart. The form and purpose of the epistles often require more explanatory language, and narratives draw us into a situation by the way the plot is structured. One style of sermon will not fit all texts.

Respecting the genre does not mean that the sermon has to be in the same genre as the text; that would be inappropriate for some texts. A sermon that denounced in the way Amos denounced would be deeply disturbing (Amos 1–2). A preacher can honour the genre of a text in a number of ways:

- By developing or following the images, style or language the author uses as appropriate and by borrowing the rhetorical impact of a text.
- By using the structure of the text, or part of it, to shape the structure of the sermon.
- By using a different but appropriate genre.

Example 1. Following the Images

In verse 4 of Psalm 23 David talks of the valley of the shadow of death. It is a valley he has walked many times in his life: facing Goliath, hunted by Saul, engaging the enemy in battle. The preacher can extend this image for there are many types of death we encounter in life: death of a loved one, death of hope, death of a relationship, death of reputation. These are all valleys of the shadow that people walk. These other instances of the 'valley of the shadow of death' can be phrased in a way that borrows the rhetorical impact of the original. The positive images from the psalm can then be developed: God as shepherd (vv 1–3), God as host of the feast, and the overflowing cup (vv 5–6).

Example 2. Using the Structure

This extract is from a sermon which uses the structure of Ruth's promise to Naomi as its structure (Ruth 1.16–17). Each section of the sermon uses a line of the promise.

Ruth stands and arches her back.
She places her hands in the small of her back and stretches.
Her back aches from working bent double.
Her fingers are cracked from the rough stalks of barley.
But it was good they arrived at harvest time,
she is fortunate to have work.
She recalls her promise:
'Where you go, I will go.'
And here she is, in a field in Bethlehem.

She thinks back to a moment she pledged herself to Naomi,
the moment she decided to leave Moab.
Moab was home, but she hardly thinks of it now.
Bethlehem is her home now and will always be so.
She will live and die here,
for that is what she promised Naomi,
'Where you die I will die and there will I be buried.'

(Sermon: *Ruth*)

Example 3. Using a Different but Appropriate Genre

A reading from an epistle could be presented in an expository manner as that is appropriate for the form. An epistle can also be presented as narrative, looking at the way three stories work together: the gospel story, the story of the recipients and the story of the writer. The following are abbreviated extracts from the three stories used in a sermon on Phil 1.1–11; 3.17–21.

> Paul's story: It is 60AD or thereabouts. Somewhere in Rome Paul is under house arrest, awaiting trial, but do not imagine some comfortable existence with just an ankle bracelet. Paul is chained and guarded. But it is better than a Roman prison. He is allowed visitors and he can write and receive letters. His life is largely one of prayer, and through prayer he brings into that small room churches from around the Roman Empire, for they are in his heart and on his mind. But Paul is still an evangelist. Old habits die hard. He spreads the gospel among the soldiers who guard him. Every time the guards change it is a chance for the next shift to overhear the gospel.
>
> The Philippians' story: The little church in Philippi in Greece needs to know how its members should live as Christians in a pagan world. Philippi is an important place with special status as a Roman town; a little bit of Italy in northern Greece. It is prosperous and well run. People are proud to be Philippians. Then a letter from Paul arrives, a really good letter, lots of rejoicing, but tucked away in it is a statement that must have caused them concern. 'Our citizenship,' says Paul, 'is in heaven and it is from there that we are expecting a saviour.' They thought they were citizens of Philippi. Paul tells them they are also citizens of heaven. They are dual nationals. How does that work? Can they still be patriotic? Can we?
>
> The gospel story: It is Christ who has made us citizens of heaven. This is not a citizenship we can apply for. It is not a citizenship we gain by being born in a particular country; it is a gift gained by what Christ has done for us. But how do we live this citizenship? Paul makes it clear that a Christian's first allegiance is to the Lord. Our primary allegiance is to God, but by being citizens of heaven first, we learn to love our country more for we are called to be good citizens (1 Pet 2.13–17). We learn to love our country so much that we are prepared to speak out when it goes wrong. That is being more patriotic, not less. If we did not care we would shut up.
>
> (Sermon: *A Tale of Two Countries*)

Engagement

How would you preach Psalm 42 in a way that honours the genre?

Honouring the genre does not replace the usual research that preachers do, it is about the way that information is used in structuring the sermon. Before consulting commentaries, immerse yourself in the psalm as a poem, allow the genre as well as the content of the psalm to shape your sermon.

A few pointers:

- The title of Psalm 42 indicates it is possibly a contemplative poem (maskil) that was sung. It is a poem for a reason so the way we preach it needs to honour that.
- Poems work by images and sound patterns to create moods. They make associations, bringing things together to create new insights or to deepen understanding.
- Images, sound patterns and associations work with the content to communicate meaning.
- Begin by reading the psalm aloud as a poem. Practice ways of presenting it orally. What will you emphasize? What will be loud? What will be quiet? Are there refrains and repetition? What patterns do they make? What is important about them?
- What images are used? How do these change? Follow the images, let them lead you through the text. What changes of mood do you detect?

Allow the answers to these questions to inform the way you structure a sermon on Psalm 42 in response to the engagement question. These questions do not lead to one style but open up different ways of honouring the genre.

Conclusion

7

The Bible is a living word through which God speaks to us. It is a presence, not an object. This puts the preacher in a personal relationship to the text, which becomes a place of encounter. In light of this, the attitudes we bring to the text and the virtues we practise become particularly important. The approaches we use should honour the nature and complexity of the text and the situations within it. In preparation preachers experience both freedom and restraint and wisely exercise 'creative fidelity' as they seek meaning.

Virtuous preachers read charitably in order to bless and build up the love of God and neighbour. They honestly face the failings as well as the achievements of biblical characters and the challenges of living as a Christian. Patience and trust are exercised concerning understanding, even if this involves 'holding your nerve' in the face of difficult texts. In order to handle the text with integrity preachers come to the Bible with humility, willing to sit under the text rather than over it but with a confidence in the text that enables them to engage with critical scholarship. Responsible wisdom and 'creative fidelity' are exercised when interpreting a text and respect is shown by the way the genre of the text informs the sermon and by the way biblical characters are depicted. The virtuous preacher is not a superhuman creature. They are someone who approaches the text with a commitment to transformation for themselves and their congregation, and practising these virtues is an important means to that end.

Bibliography

The following resources are helpful for thinking further about this subject. The work of Richard Briggs and Kevin Vanhoozer underpins much of what I have written. Other works tackle issues such as how preachers use imagination, how we handle difficult texts and how we can reveal the relevance of a text and God's action in the now.

R S Briggs, *The Virtuous Reader: Old Testament Narrative and Interpretive Virtue* (Grand Rapids, MI: Baker Academic, 2010)

K Bruce, *Igniting the Heart: Preaching and Imagination* (London: SCM Press, 2015)

K Bruce and J Harrison (eds), *Wrestling with the Word: Preaching Tricky Texts* (London: SPCK, 2016)

M Cooling, *Preaching That Shows: Revealing Relevance* (London: SCM, 2022)

A M McKenzie, *Making a Scene in the Pulpit: Vivid Preaching for Visual Listeners* (Louisville, KY: Westminster John Knox Press, 2018)

P K Stevenson, *Preaching*, SCM Study Guide (London: SCM, 2017)

L Shercliff and M Allen, *The Present Preacher: Discerning God in the Now* (Norwich: Canterbury Press, 2021)

K Vanhoozer, *Is There a Meaning in this Text?* (Leicester: Apollos, 1998) (see particularly chapter 7)

Notes

1 K Vanhoozer, *Is There a Meaning in this Text?* (Leicester: Apollos, 1998) pp 140, 204–207, 301, 346–350, 367–441.

2 R S Briggs, *The Virtuous Reader: Old Testament Narrative and Interpretive Virtue* (Grand Rapids, MI: Baker Academic, 2010) pp 60–69, 96–100, 130–133, 140–145, 161–166, 187–192.

3 J Bell, 'Psalm 137' in K Bruce and J Harrison (eds), *Wrestling with the Word: Preaching Tricky Texts* (London: SPCK, 2016) pp 45–49.

4 M A Powell, *What Do They Hear?: Bridging the Gap Between Pulpit and Pew* (Nashville, TN: Abingdon Press, 2007).

5 Vanhoozer, *Meaning, op cit*, pp 228–229, 301.

6 L Newbigin, *Proper Confidence* (London: SPCK, 1995) p 105.

7 Briggs, *Virtuous Reader, op cit*, pp 179, 188.

8 W C Booth, *The Company We Keep* (Oakland: University of California Press, 1992) pp 169–178, 221–223.

9 Vanhoozer, *Meaning, op cit*, pp 388, 407.

10 N T Wright, *Luke For Everyone* (London: SPCK, 2004) pp 130–131.

11 Briggs, *Virtuous Reader, op cit*, p 99.

12 Briggs, *Virtuous Reader, op cit*, p 97.